HOLDING the REINS

A RIDE THROUGH COWGIRL LIFE

By **Marc Talbert**

Photographs by
Barbara Van Cleve

HarperCollins *Publishers*

Talbert, Marc.   Holding the reins : a ride through cowgirl life : by Marc Talbert ; photographs by Barbara Van Cleve.   p.   cm.
Summary: Explores a year in the life of four teenage cowgirls as they live and work on their home ranches in Utah, Colorado, Montana,
Wyoming, and New Mexico.   ISBN 0-06-029255-5 — ISBN 0-06-029256-3 (lib. bdg.)
1. Cowgirls—West (U.S.)—Social life and customs—Juvenile literature.   2. Ranch life—West (U.S.)—Juvenile literature.
3. West (U.S.)—Social life and customs—Juvenile literature.   4. Cowgirls—West (U.S.)—Biography—Juvenile literature.
5. Teenage girls—West (U.S.)—Biography—Juvenile literature.   6. West (U.S.)—Biography—Juvenile literature.
[1. Cowgirls.   2. Ranch life—West (U.S.)   3. West (U.S.)—Social life and customs.   4. West (U.S.)—Biography.
5. Women–Biography.]   I. Van Cleve, Barbara, 1935–   II. Title.
F596 .T35   2003   978—dc21   2002068734   CIP   AC   Typography by Carla Weise   1 2 3 4 5 6 7 8 9 10   ❖   First Edition

For Lois and Jerry Morel

with love and gratitude

And in memory of Hazel Long

—M.T.

For my father, Spike,

who raised his ranch daughters to believe

we could do anything if we worked hard.

He taught us to see the beauty in ranching life,

to appreciate and respect animals,

to enjoy and cherish family,

and to share with our community.

—B.V.C.

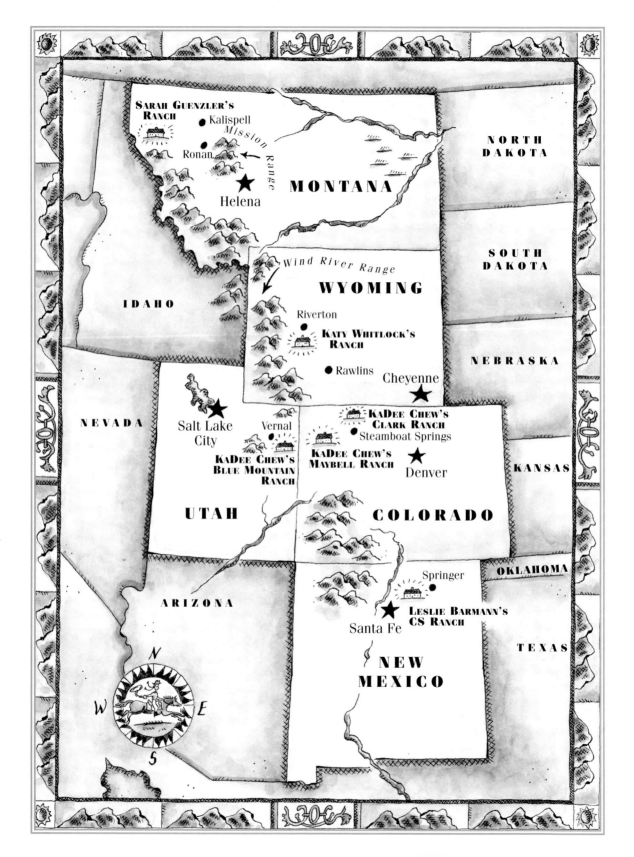

CONTENTS

INTRODUCTION

W HEN I WAS A BOY, and living in the Midwest, I dreamed about being a cowboy. Every Saturday morning I watched cowboy shows on our television—Roy Rogers, the Lone Ranger. There was always lots of gunplay and fancy horseback riding. If there was singing, I waited patiently until it was over. There were good guys and bad guys—and the good guys always won. I'd wear my false-leather chaps and my false-metal six-shooter and my no-scuff plastic cowboy boots and sprawl on the floor and let the television story stampede over me.

Now that I live in the West—in an area where some of those shows were actually filmed—I don't dream of being a cowboy anymore. For one thing, I'm a little old for all of that. Besides, I know that being a working cowboy on a real ranch is harder work than anything I saw on those television shows, harder work than I'd like to do day in and day out, through all the seasons of the year.

But not too long ago, at a real ranch in real ranching country, I found myself watching some cattle being herded. I couldn't help wishing I'd given my cowboy dreams a little more rein, taken them a little more seriously. The horses and riders looked so sure of themselves,

and so good at what they were doing. What they were doing looked like lots of serious fun.

Off in the distance I saw a horse and rider heading off a bolting calf. Some things about real-life ranching haven't changed in over a hundred years, and this is one of them: calves breaking away from the herd and being brought back to it.

The horse and rider were good. The rider's reins were comfortably loose, and the horse responded quickly and calmly to the rider's invisible commands. The rider sat tall in the saddle, moving gracefully in ways that matched the movements of the horse. It looked as if they were dancing. As horse and rider drew near, I squinted. Was that a ponytail bouncing from behind the hat?

It was.

Times have changed, and some cowboys have ponytails even though Roy Rogers did not. I looked closer. The rider wasn't a cowboy, but a cowgirl.

How stupid did I feel? Plenty. I've lived in ranching country long enough to know that somebody wearing a cowboy hat and sitting on a horse isn't necessarily a guy.

There have always been cowgirls—girls and women who herded and roped and flanked and branded and did anything else that the boys and men did—even if I didn't see them on television when I was a kid,

or read about them, or listen to songs celebrating them.

If you don't believe this, go to any family ranch today and you'll see girls who live and work alongside their parents and brothers and the hired hands, doing anything and everything that needs to be done. They are good at whatever it takes to be a rancher. And what's more, they are good at whatever other girls all over this country love to do—whether that is sewing or cooking or dressing fancy and feminine or tuning car engines.

I may not dream about being a cowboy these days, but I have two daughters and they dream about being a lot of things I never saw girls doing when I was a boy. As their father, I want them to be anything they want to be. And whatever they become, I'd like them to have an attitude like that of the cowgirl I mistook for a cowboy: holding the reins with confidence, sitting deep in the saddle, head high, in control, female and proud. Like that cowgirl, I'd like my girls to look toward futures that are big and open and just this side of being tamed.

Such a future sounds like ranch country to me.

So give your horse a little more rein, and nudge him with your heels. Let's go for a ride through the seasons of a ranch year. There are four cowgirls waiting for us over that rise, and we need to catch up to them.

Marc Talbert

SUMMER IS A PLACE
KaDee Chew, Utah and Colorado

MOST OF US think of summer as a time of the year. Indeed, it is a big old hot-breathed chunk of time, but for ranching families summer can also be a place.

In the case of KaDee Chew's family, summer is three places.

"There's Blue Mountain," says KaDee, as she sits on the horizontal length of a pole fence, facing the empty sheep corral on Blue Mountain, "and Maybell and Clark." She is a young woman of few words, but all of them mean something.

For KaDee, summer starts here at Blue Mountain, which straddles the north end of the border that separates Utah from Colorado. For someone looking over the swales and hillocks of Blue Mountain's sprawling top, dividing this land into separate states makes as much sense as dividing the sky into north and south using the fast-fading contrail of a jet going from Denver to Salt Lake City.

This is, after all, a land where some horses bear striped scars across their shoulders and haunches from the claws of mountain lions.

For KaDee Chew, summer means moving among her family's three ranches.

This is, after all, a land where herds of Mormon crickets—grasshoppers in ill-fitting cricketlike armor—march across the summer landscape, making the ground itself look as if it were moving and making trucks fishtail on roads that are slimy with their squished bodies.

This is a land that has outlasted dinosaurs by hundreds of millions of years, a land that hoards the bones of those creatures in its rock. In fact, Dinosaur National Monument, which celebrates such remnants of extinction, forms boundaries with the Chew Ranch along its western, northern, and eastern edges. The Chews hope the ranching way of life doesn't go the way of the dinosaurs, or that anyone would celebrate its extinction if that happened.

This is a land that endures, and so do the people who call it home. Homesteader cabins, some of which may have been visited by such cattle-rustling outlaws as Butch Cassidy and the Sundance Kid from nearby Brown's Park, still dot the landscape, some of them leaning away from the wind or sagging, but standing nonetheless. These homesteads of 640 acres were cobbled together over time into the larger ranches that exist now. The toughest ranchers remain.

"I can't imagine living anyplace else," KaDee shrugs, flashing a smile. She is descended from these homesteaders, a product of the land. "I don't like being in large crowds . . . you know, twenty people or more . . . especially if I don't know any of them." She is standing next to the corral now and looking through a notch in the landscape where two staggered hills barely overlap. Thirty miles away, and framed in this notch as if in the sight of a rifle, is Vernal's four-lane Main Street, pale as the underbelly of a dead snake stretched out in the sun. Lights wink off the windshields of cars coming straight toward her.

KaDee is a rare thing: a teenager who prefers the solitude of Blue Mountain to the relative bustle of Vernal. But that doesn't make her unsophisticated by any means. She has worn the blue satin–twinklecloth prom dress she made herself, combining several different patterns, with

KaDee and her mother, Grace, show off KaDee's handiwork.

the same easy confidence and style as the jeans and cowboy shirt she wears to ride her horse or feed the chickens.

Like KaDee, Blue Mountain is a rare thing: a mountain leaning toward one side, frozen in the act of rearing up from the Green River Valley where the Yampa River flows into it. Blue Mountain's peaks point south, and eventually their flanks run flush into a high desert of sagebrush and sandstone, blue clay and red-rock rubble.

At two hundred feet shy of eight thousand feet in elevation, Blue Mountain is part of what KaDee's grandfather, Dean Chew (known as DadDean by the family), calls their "intermediate" ranch. As such, it is good for both sheep and cattle in three seasons of most years.

Sheep are the focus today, and sheep are close to the heart of every Chew. "Whatever we got now," says DadDean, peering from under his floppy-brimmed cowboy hat, "we got because of the sheep."

Why does KaDee like sheep better than cattle? "Well, when you have trouble with a cow, they're so big you can get hurt," she says. "Sheep are smaller, so when you have trouble with a sheep, you just laugh and straighten it out."

In a couple of hours the corrals that lie empty will be filled with over six hundred black-faced lambs, plus their mothers. Today is docking day, and KaDee's parents and two brothers, one uncle, several cousins, and

two hired hands will be plenty busy working on lambs that range from one to five weeks in age.

The Chews raise both black-faced Suffolk sheep and white Columbia/Rambouillet crossbred sheep. They keep each type of sheep in separate pastures and raise them for different reasons. The black-faced lambs are raised for meat and the white sheep for wool. As sheep go, they have distinct personalities, black-faced ewes being more independent and feisty, white ewes being more protective of their lambs and more prone to stay in tight flocks. Also, black-faced ewes often have twins and sometimes triplets, while white ewes most often have single lambs, with occasional twins.

"Here they come," says KaDee, looking toward the road. And sure enough, a flock of sheep is ambling toward the corrals, several of them pausing to nip at stalks of grass, the lambs bleating and panting to keep up. On horseback, behind these moving lumps of fleece, are KaDee's mother, Grace; her father, Alan; her brothers, Quayle and Jacob; and her cousins, MarLynn and Justin. On the saddle, on his lap, KaDee's father holds a lamb that was too young to keep up with the flock.

The family's dogs help control the edges of the flock, but the horses and riders keep the sheep moving.

KaDee opens gates for the sheep, which wander into the holding

Sheep run, hop, and skip into the holding pen.

pen. Ushering them in, she moves in such a way that it becomes obvious she knows what the sheep are going to do before they even move. The sheep gravitate toward thin strips of shade made by the pen's southern fence, a combination of slats and upright poles set shoulder to shoulder, known as a slab fence. KaDee's uncle Neil, who has been waiting with KaDee, has sharpened his knife and is ready to be in charge of what comes next: docking.

What is docking? KaDee thinks for a moment. "It's when you cut off

the tails and brand and vaccinate, and then, if it's a male, you castrate."

Every ranch does it a little differently, and the Chew family does it differently depending on how early or late the lambs are born. KaDee makes docking sound simple enough, and the Chew family makes it look simple—even though it is not.

From the larger flock, small bunches of ewes and lambs are separated into a narrow, alleylike chute. Five or six people in the chute wade among the sheep, lifting lambs up to the top of the fence and presenting them, bottom first, to Neil and Alan in the adjacent corral. Sheep become surprisingly docile when made to "sit" on the small of their backs. The lambs' hind legs are held up, exposing tails, rumps, and genitals.

KaDee steps forward with the vaccine gun, sticks the needle in the rump to her left, and squeezes with her trigger finger. What she injects into each lamb's muscle is not an antibiotic or vitamins, but a serum that prevents lambs from overeating when they begin grazing more and nursing less. The best eaters will sometimes wither away because of intestinal problems caused by eating too much forage.

She moves on to the other lambs being held on top of the fence. A docker, either Neil or Alan, steps up to take her place.

With one swift movement of his knife, the docker cuts off the end of the lamb's tail, between one half and two thirds of its length, just below

where it looks "meaty." A thin but intense stream of blood shoots from the stub, often hitting the docker on the chest or arm.

If the lamb is a female, the docker has finished cutting. The lamb is carefully rolled forward off the small of its back and lowered into the corral on all four legs. Two of KaDee's younger cousins have been standing by with the sheep brands—large wooden sticks carved on the bottom end into a diamond shape and dipped into red paint. The paint smells like ordinary oil-based house paint, but it is a special sheep-branding paint made with lanolin, the oil found in wool. With both hands, they press the diamond shape between the lamb's shoulder blades. The trick is to get more branding paint on the lambs than on themselves. Sometimes this goal is not met.

The branded lamb will often leap about the corral or wander, dazed, looking for its mother. In all of this, the lamb seems to suffer most from being separated from its mother. If a lamb finds her right away, it begins nursing, seemingly unaware that its docked tail is still dripping blood.

If the lamb is male, the docker must do more cutting. He bunches up the scrotum with one hand, cutting it open with the other. When the sharp-ended testicles pop partway out, he bows his head to secure them

Older brother Jacob presents a lamb for KaDee's vaccine gun.

gently but firmly with his teeth, which frees the knifeless hand to grasp them. Instead of cutting the thin cords that connect the testicles to the animal's sexual plumbing, he pulls them until they break. This way, Neil explains, there is less bleeding and less chance of a knife slipping and cutting something it shouldn't in castration. The young lambs seem unaware of what has just happened.

But the cutting is still not finished. After the male lamb is carefully lowered to the ground, and while the brand is being applied, the docker folds the tip of its left ear lengthwise and cuts it off. Anyone will now be able to tell at a glance, because of the notched ear, that this is a male.

In spite of all the cutting, there is very little blood near the fence or on the lambs themselves. Instead, little piles of testicles begin to form where they are thrown, and larger piles of tails. At the end of the day, the testicles will be gathered together for burying—to prevent coyotes or other scavengers from feasting on them and then developing a taste for lamb. The tails will be buried too, for the same reason, but they will be counted first—laid out in piles of ten. This is the only way to know for certain how many lambs have been docked on any given day.

As the morning progresses, the corral begins to fill and the holding pen begins to look empty. With such a big sky, the sun seems to have to work harder moving from east to west, and like anything else that works

KaDee counts lamb tails before dropping them into a bag for burial.

hard, it has grown hotter with the effort. The wind kicks up, making things cooler, but at a price—dust collects on sweaty faces, necks, and arms.

Why go to the trouble of cutting off each lamb's tail?

"Fly blow," the family answers, almost in one voice. Lambs don't lift their tails enough to clear them of feces and urine. Tails, cute as they are at first, can become caked with a fecal icing that attracts flies, which lay

eggs in it. Maggots hatching from the eggs sometimes burrow into the flesh of the tail. From there they can be carried through the blood toward the lamb's internal organs, which can become infected. This can kill the lamb.

But the Chews don't always cut off the tails. Sometimes, triggered by weather, lambs are born earlier in the year. Because they (and their tails) are larger at docking time, and consequently bleed more heavily, the Chews sometimes band their tails instead of cutting them off. To do this, they stretch a special kind of rubber band over the tail's joint where it would be cut. "Cutting is probably less painful," says KaDee. "Banding is like having a rubber band around your finger, cutting off the blood. It'll begin to hurt." She smiles, and then apologizes for this smile with a shrug. "When they're banded they will be just standing there, and suddenly they'll jump straight up, almost doing a back flip. It looks funny, even though it's not. The pain makes 'em do it."

Banding was common among sheep ranchers when very short tails were in fashion; they enhanced the size of a sheep's hindquarters. Cutting was more dangerous then because ranchers would cut tails so short that some lambs would bleed to death. But banding causes no bleeding and doesn't attract flies to fresh or scabbed blood. The tails simply die, dry up, and fall off.

Fashions in ranching change with the times. Moderately short tails are most common now, so the Chews are banding sheep less and less.

Why were sheep born with long tails to begin with, if fly blow is the likely result?

Each Chew has a slightly different answer. But after airing different opinions, they arrive at a single plausible answer. Various lines of domestic sheep have been bred for thousands of years without regard to tail length. Wild sheep, such as bighorn sheep, tend to have naturally shorter tails.

KaDee should know. Later that evening, after a long day of docking, she returns to Chew Ranch headquarters outside of Jensen, thirteen miles from Vernal, to tend a special little bunch of sheep. Late last fall, a wild bighorn ram settled in among a flock of black-faced sheep. Four of the lambs he sired survived—remarkably, because the gestation period in a black-faced ewe is five months, compared with seven months for a bighorn ewe. In other words, each of these lambs was born two months premature, with lung problems that required special care and medication. KaDee and her family are raising them as an experiment to see how robust these crossbred sheep grow to be.

The half-wild lambs are excellent climbers and have brown hair that is less nappy than that of fullbred black-faced sheep. They seem to have more teeth in their narrower mouths. And they naturally have shorter

tails than their black-faced cousins. KaDee can also feel nubs on either side of their foreheads, between their ears—the beginnings of horns.

"Cute, aren't they?" she says, watching them kick up their heels while they dance around their black-faced mothers.

• • •

Almost one hundred miles to the east, straddling the Yampa River, is the Chew family's spread outside of Maybell, Colorado. The flat, narrow river valley is irrigated, its fields of hay perpetually green in the summer. There is so little movement that this landscape might just be an oversized photograph, freezing this place in a blink of time.

However, this illusion is broken by a hawk wheeling overhead, below a galloping herd of wispy clouds.

Maybell is like an echo of Jensen and Blue Mountain. Its landscape is similar, but gentler and less rugged. Branding cattle and docking sheep on Blue Mountain take place at the beginning of June. In Maybell they will happen in mid-June.

And where are the sheep and cattle shipped to?

As the hawk flies, not that far, but to a world apart: the Chews' third summer ranch in Clark, Colorado, twenty miles north of Steamboat

KaDee scoops up a lamb that has wandered away from its mother.

Springs, one of Colorado's busiest ski resorts, almost on the Wyoming border.

"Everything ends up in Clark every summer," KaDee says. By that she means sheep and cattle. And herself.

The Chews' Clark ranch is made up of several alpine shelves of land rising from the Elk River Valley, each shelf draped with mountain meadows that are surrounded by stands of aspen. It is easy to see why so many outsiders shell out big bucks to buy ranches here in order to build huge trophy homes of massive logs and native boulders and to dabble in horses or sheep or cattle, or even llamas.

For some landowners, it would be hard to pass up the big money a magnificent high-altitude ranch would command on the booming real estate market. For the Chews, it would be much harder to abandon the way of life their ranch makes possible. The Chews will be here long after most of the newcomers are gone, replaced by other newcomers who haven't experienced a typical annual snowfall that is so deep it collapses fences and lingers through May.

Summer will find KaDee living on the Clark ranch and doing any number of things—fishing, picking wildflowers, taking photographs with her mother's camera for a 4-H project, shooting at varmints such as skunks or coyotes with her rifle. But the bulk of her time will be spent on

horseback—keeping track of cattle and sheep—or inside the cab of a truck or on a tractor. She drives the tractor that cuts, rakes, and bales hay and then loads it onto flatbed trailers hauled by the truck.

On any given summer day, you might glimpse her on horseback, her hand ready to grab her rifle from its saddle scabbard as she meanders through scenery that could be from *The Sound of Music*—spectacular, seemingly untouched by humans. If she is behind the wheel of a truck, KaDee will be listening to her favorite country music station on the radio, definitely not Rodgers and Hammerstein. Reception is as clear as the blue sky over the mountains across the way. As she listens, she dreams of owning her own Ford truck, all fixed up with a music system and plenty of horsepower.

"I love to daydream," KaDee admits. And what a place for day-dreaming! As birds pop right and left from the grass in front of her, she can daydream about growing plants in a greenhouse with her mother or making clothes with her aunt Renee. She can daydream about going to the movies with friends in Vernal or western swing-dancing with a boy who may or may not have a late seventies Ford pickup—a '79 is her favorite.

She can daydream about a baby kitten back in Jensen cautiously trying to steal a chicken bone from its mother, or about those half-wild

lambs with the short tails, or about winning a blue ribbon for her 4-H ewe at the Routt County Fair in Steamboat Springs, or about the classes she'll take next year in high school in Vernal. She can daydream about what new welded sculpture she'll make or what she'll sketch next in pencil and charcoal, or about being a veterinarian's assistant after she graduates from high school, or about working her own ranch.

There is a lot to daydream about. But when it comes time to concentrate on helping load huge round bales of hay, KaDee is all business. Hay certified by the county extension agent is weed-free and is bound in two-stranded orange-and-blue twine. Such hay is slightly more valuable—hunters and packers are required to use it in the wilderness so as not to spread noxious weeds. Plain orange twine binds noncertified hay. The two types of hay are loaded separately.

KaDee can position the truck perfectly for the tractor as its front-loading fork lowers the massive bales. The lines of her rows don't wobble when she drives the tractor that rakes hay into long, yarnlike piles.

KaDee is helping her uncle Neil load hay in a high field at four in the afternoon in late summer when her mother checks on her. "I haven't had lunch yet," KaDee says. There wasn't time that morning to fix anything, she explains, and there's been no break in working that would

The windrows of hay KaDee makes stretch out behind her as straight and neat as thick yarn.

allow her to drive for a half hour back down to the Clark ranch head-quarters. When her mother expresses dismay that KaDee missed a meal, KaDee shrugs and almost smiles. "Don't worry. Just a couple

more bales and I can go down." She does, however, accept the offer of a soda, warm from sitting in her mother's truck all day.

KaDee hands back the empty soda bottle, rolls up the window for the benefit of air-conditioning, and swings the truck and its trailer wide, following the tractor as it bounces along the edge of the field.

Summer is a place, and KaDee is exactly where she belongs.

KaDee hops from the swather after cutting a field of hay at her family's Clark ranch.

JUGGLING THE BUSYNESS OF FALL
Sarah Guenzler, Montana

SOME YEARS, fall in the Mission Valley of northwest Montana seems to come on the thundering feet of a local herd of stampeding buffalo. This year, on the Guenzler family ranch just west of Ronan, fall seems to have come on the careful, light feet of the white-tailed deer that haunt nearby swales and windbreaks. One day the naked peaks of the Mission Range mountains to the east had plum-colored shadows. The next day, these shadows were steel blue and the mountains' rocky spikes were covered with snow.

Regardless of how fall comes, the dark of night breaks up later each morning, which doesn't stop Sarah Guenzler and her younger brother, Levi, from rising at their usual time, six o'clock—there are chores to be done before school. Early as that is, they aren't the first ones up each weekday morning. Their mother, Sharon, was up a couple of hours earlier and is at work in town, helping prepare breakfast for all the students in Ronan. Their father, Paul, isn't bed ballast any later than his wife. He's out doing chores, taking the measure of the day.

Sarah Guenzler loves the busyness of her many jobs.

Sarah steps outside from the brightly lit kitchen and pauses for a moment, letting her eyes get used to the predawn gloom. As her eyes adjust, she looks toward a flock of nearly fifty ducks in a pond that lies in the draw between her house and the barn. The cuticle of ice around the pond no longer melts during the day. It has grown outward from the bank, thickening into a shelf the dogs can walk on. The ducks are clumped together, slowly rotating in the water, keeping the ice from advancing. Fall is a time for many animals and people to reestablish communities, which help to keep the darkness and the cold at bay.

Sarah is carrying big bottles capped with red rubber teats and heavy with warm formula. The air is filled with the bawling of cows—a bunch of calves were weaned yesterday, separated from their mothers, whose maternal instincts and full udders urge them to keep searching for their offspring.

As Sarah walks toward the barn, several goats appear, filling the air with their strong, sweet scent. They dance on mud that is stiff with cold but not hard, feeling like chilled cookie dough underfoot, and just as sticky and crumbly. Sarah shoos them away as she slides open the big barn door. One begins to nibble at her gloves. "They're after some grain,"

Sarah has her hands full of breakfast for three calves.

she says. "But they'll eat anything." The goat has mischief in his eyes, which peer at her through pupils that are vertical slits instead of round dots.

Sarah brushes the goat aside and flips on the barn lights, a string of lightbulbs tacked to the ceiling and leading to a stall where three calves peer at her through the slats. Their noses are dripping, their eyes showing white with anticipation. These are calves that will be used by her family for practicing breakaway roping come spring.

Sarah squeezes through the slats and clamps a bottle under each elbow. She positions them at just the right angle, forcing the calves to lower their necks and tip their heads up—good posture for nursing. Holding on to the bottles can be tricky—the calves occasionally butt at them, just as they did with their mothers, trying to bring down more milk, to make it flow faster down their throats. The stall fills with the sloppy sounds of sucking.

The bottles are soon empty. One calf has a cap of milk between its ears, from when the nipple flipped out of its mouth and squirted it. Sarah watches the calves lick the rings of formula from around their mouths, the pointy tips of their tongues flicking in and out of their nostrils. "Look

Breakfast is served!

at how long their tongues are," she says, turning to measure out some grain for them.

Just as she's ready to leave, Levi appears at the doorway. He's come to fetch feed for the flock of chickens and turkeys that he keeps safe from coyotes and foxes in a newer, shorter barn a couple dozen yards farther from the house. None of the turkeys are reserved for Thanksgiving, which is fast approaching. The turkeys are pets.

The calves fed, Sarah closes the barn door and makes a short detour to look in on several mares and colts in a paddock across from the barn. Her family has between forty and fifty horses, which it breeds for use on the ranch and to sell. A couple of them are Sarah's. She doesn't get an allowance, but she can keep the money she earns from selling any of the horses (or cattle) that belong to her. So far she's put most of that money aside for college.

This collection of colts she's looking at includes a Shetland pony/ quarter horse cross, not exactly working ranch stock. "They sell real well," Sarah explains. Indeed, this Shetland cross is as cute as a plush hobbyhorse and already showing evidence of the distinctively ornery, but winning, Shetland pony personality.

The mares and colts are doing fine. One colt is tame enough to approach Sarah, presenting its neck and the underside of its jaw for a

scratch. It is important for colts to feel comfortable around people—the younger they are when they learn this, the better. Above the sound of the cows calling for their calves, a truck engine rumbles to life. Sarah's father is warming the truck to drive Sarah and Levi a mile or so to the bus stop at the mouth of Guenzler Road. The outside working dog begins to bark and leap in the air, begging to be taken off the rope that anchors him to his doghouse, eager for his working day to start.

Back inside, Sarah and Levi rummage through the bedroom they share to assemble what they need for school. The house dogs watch them from under the kitchen table. A tailless cat lies curled in the seat of a kitchen chair. "Let's go!" their father calls.

Fall is a time when the day speeds along almost too fast for anyone to feel the bumps. It's a time when the sunlight grows so dim that it seems always to be filtered through the dirt-dusted windows of the pickup truck that trails skirts of dust as it rumbles toward the bus stop.

"Have a good day!" Paul calls as Sarah and Levi tumble from the truck, which does a gravel-crunching three-point turn and roars back toward the ranch. Today Paul and his hired hand, Jake, will be setting fence posts along the boundaries of a piece of land the Guenzlers bought earlier in the year, stitching their ranch together with wood and wire.

Sarah and Levi walk along Guenzler Road on their way to school.

Sarah and Levi walk to where Guenzler Road feeds into pavement.
They wait. It seems oddly quiet—from this spot they can't hear the cows
calling for their weaned calves. At this time of the year there are no song-
birds to break the morning stillness. Behind them, beyond town, lies the
Mission Range. Ordinarily, the teeth of these mountains comb thin

breezes that surge from the west. Today they are snagged on a layer of wooly clouds.

Sarah pricks up her ears. "It's coming," she says. The bus pops up from the rise and wheezes to a stop. The door snaps open, and Sarah and Levi climb aboard.

• • •

What do you call a large collection of middle-school kids? A flock? A herd? A gaggle? A rabble? A pack? Whatever you choose to call them, the kids at the Ronan Middle School form a community that, more or less, has been together since first grade. As glorious as summer on a family ranch can be, Sarah looks forward to school and fall. Why? "I get to see my friends," she says, with a look that seems to add, "Simple as that."

The middle school at Ronan is a diverse community. Ronan and the Guenzler ranch, which was homesteaded by Sarah's great-great-grandparents in 1910, lie near the heart of the Flathead Indian Reservation. About half the students at Sarah's middle school represent fifty-two different Native American tribes from around the country, including the local Salish and Kootenai Indians. Many of their relatives are students and faculty of the nearby Salish-Kootenai College.

Even though the Ronan School District draws from a large area surrounding Ronan, Sarah goes to school with relatively few kids who work

on ranches. Many privately held pieces of land within the Reservation, like the Guenzler ranch, are slowly being carved up into "ranchettes," whose inhabitants don't live off the land, but instead work in surrounding towns. And because of the gently rolling terrain and healthy topsoil that blankets the Mission Valley, much of the land isn't ranched, but farmed instead—for potatoes in particular.

Sarah laughs and talks and navigates comfortably around students milling through the halls before the first bell rings. There is no hint of uneasiness as she makes her way to the cafeteria to say a quick hello to her mother. She seems perfectly comfortable in the angular, noisy, seemingly chaotic atmosphere of school—and she is. One wouldn't know that Sarah feels, in some ways, that she leads a double life, that she lives in two distinct, sometimes contradictory, worlds.

One world is that of a rancher. In this world, during the fall, she contributes by doing all her usual chores *plus* helping her family ship cattle, pregnancy-test cows, and vaccinate cattle and horses. She also practices barrel racing and breakaway calf-roping at an indoor ring in nearby Kalispell, and hunts deer with her father in the tall ponderosa and spruce stands near her family's summer ranch outside of Thompson Falls to the northwest.

The second world in which she lives is that of an eighth-grader. In

Sarah's other life—as a middle-school student.

this world she sings in the choir, plays basketball (as number 45, she
helped her girls team win the regionals), attends 4-H meetings, and
makes top grades in literature, algebra, social studies, Spanish, English,
and science. She may be a rancher, but Sarah fits right in with all the
other town-oriented eighth-graders.

Sarah is not a flashy dresser. She's changed the pants she wore while doing her chores earlier, but her jacket shows faint evidence of her having worked with animals. Yet she radiates a quiet confidence, seeming almost serene in the midst of the slow-motion riot that is school. A variety of students, both boys and girls, seek her company. Her teachers, some of whom taught her parents when they were in junior high, treat her with the same respect she shows them.

Does ranch life encourage the kind of confidence and self-respect that leads to respecting others? Looking at Sarah mingling and socializing with people at school, one is tempted to say that it does.

Later in the morning, Sarah returns to her locker. She opens it and there, taped to the inside of the door, at eye level, is an oversized color photograph. It is a reminder of her other world. In the photo, she is kneeling with her father and one of their dogs behind her first buck, which is laid out on the ground and gutted. Sarah is holding his head up by the antlers, which cradle her six-millimeter bolt-action rifle. The picture was taken two years ago, and Sarah is hoping to take another buck this year. Time is running out—there are only two more weekends left in hunting season.

This fall day speeds along, even though substitute teachers greet Sarah and her classmates in a couple of classes. This break in school

routine is disconcerting, and it is a relief to hear the bell announcing lunch.

The lunch line moves quickly. Sarah says another hello-in-passing to her mother. The lunch—turkey in gravy with mashed potatoes—goes down easily. And then it's outside for recess.

Stoked with food, Sarah and a group of girls shed their jackets and begin playing one-hoop basketball on an asphalt court. During the game, various girls apologize for sloppy passing or for messing up a play. When Sarah shoots, she usually makes a basket. But she puts most of her effort into setting up plays rather than grandstanding. The way she participates has roots in ranch life, where the importance of the individual and that of teamwork are carefully balanced as a matter of survival.

The girls are soon joined by some boys, and the nature of the game changes. It is boys against girls, and there is no time for apologies. In eighth grade the boys have a height advantage, which seems to inspire tighter teamwork among the girls.

Sarah continues to make plays, passing to teammates who are open, shooting only when she is in a good position. The boys take shots from anywhere and everywhere, banking the ball off the chain link fence behind the hoop, stutter-dribbling and passing the ball from between their legs—seemingly more concerned about executing fancy moves than making baskets. This works in the girls' favor, and the scoring is nearly

even. Sarah and the other girls are not pushovers. After fifteen minutes, the intensity of the game fades. Both boys and girls relax and, for one boy-girl couple, there are several instances of the "hugging" defense. The bell rings and the pile of jackets disappears as everyone goes inside. Next on Sarah's agenda: choir.

As it warms up, the choir sounds like a pack of coyotes attempting opera. Sarah's teacher, Ms. Gilhouse, walks up and down the rows, gently tapping various choir members in the tummy to remind them to tighten their diaphragms, which improves sound as well as posture. After a few minutes, with live piano accompaniment, the blended sounds that come from their properly focused diaphragms and their O-shaped mouths become rounded, full, and pleasing.

And then it is off to Spanish, where there is a quiz on body parts and, no, "elbow" does not become *el bow* in Spanish, even in Montana, where these kids are so far from Mexico and so close to Canada. Science class rounds out the school day.

During a Montana fall, as the bus leaves, the dark of night begins to return, making the sky-blue water tower in Pablo, ten miles away, seem to sink into the fields and pastures and windbreaks stretching

Sarah dribbles before passing the ball to an open teammate.

across the valley. The bus lets them off where it picked them up that morning. This time Sarah and Levi walk home. The bawling of bereft cows grows louder as they near the house and barns.

Dogs greet them. Goats suddenly appear. Chores await, balancing this end of the day with morning. It's Friday, so homework can wait a day.

Once more, Sarah and her brother have made a successful transition from the world of school to the world of the ranch. They have left the community of fellow students behind and rejoined the collection of animals their family cares for, the collection of buildings and hills Sarah calls home.

• • •

Weekends are a grab bag of activity. This Saturday, after morning chores, some horses must be inoculated against respiratory infections and worms. A bucket of grain helps Sarah catch them for haltering, after which Sarah and her mother measure doses of serum into syringes. One by one, the needles go into the fleshy area near the crest of the horse's neck, one inoculation on each side. Some horses dislike this more than others, throwing their heads at the mere glint of the syringe.

"I think I started pushing down before I got the needle in," Sarah

Sarah inoculates the family's Shetland pony/quarter horse cross.

calls to her mother, after trying to inoculate an especially edgy horse.

"I think she got enough," Sharon replies as she points a syringe toward the sky and then flicks an air bubble upward so she can squeeze it from the needle.

Back at the house, Sarah helps Levi with his math homework while Sharon makes lunch—sloppy joes. Levi quietly enjoys his sister's confusion. Sixth-grade work is surprisingly tricky from the distance of eighth grade. Sarah does her best to appear all-knowing. But this brother and sister know and, for the most part, like each other too well for one to fool the other. Paul and Jake come in from their fence work. Over lunch, conversation ranges from hunting to horses to cats, with plenty of laughter stringing the stories together.

After lunch, the horses that were inoculated must be moved to a pasture a mile or so away. This will be Sarah and Levi's job. They saddle up their own horses and, one on each flank, begin pushing this small herd along. The Shetland mare, mother of the Shetland/quarter horse cross, trots along. Nobody has bothered (or, perhaps, dared) to tell her that she is half the size of the other horses. She keeps up, her legs a blur compared with those of her companions.

It is suddenly time for afternoon chores. Levi carries some of the eggs he's collected from his chickens. As usual, one of the many eggs is

Sarah and Levi head home after moving some horses to another pasture.

green and another is blue, having come from breeds that lay such colored eggs. He hands those to Sarah. Their colors are special, but that is not what Sarah appreciates about them. "I just love the way they feel," she says. She holds up her right hand. "And this one is warmer than the other," she adds, letting the eggs nest in her palms.

As Sarah and Levi walk from the barn to the house, the darkness seems to rise from the ground, fogging the night air.

• • •

Sunday morning means getting ready for a barrel-racing competition in Kalispell. But first Sarah and her brother join one set of grandparents at church in nearby Polson. Sarah and Levi don't go every Sunday. "But I believe in the Lord," Sarah says. "And I'm glad to be in the outdoors He made for us."

She moves as comfortably in church as she does in school, and nearly everybody knows her and greets her. This is yet another community Sarah belongs to—along with 4-H and the basketball team. Belonging to so many communities is to juggle many roles, sometimes all at the same time.

In church Sarah sings with the same poise as in her school choir. During the sermon, she sits with the same respect she shows in her eighth-grade classes.

Back home, Sarah fixes her hair for the competition in Kalispell. To keep it out of her way, she pulls it back from her forehead and binds it tightly with ties of many colors into a dozen miniature and interconnecting ponytails. All of the hair ties will be hidden under her cowboy hat. The only hair that will show will be the long fringe flowing from the back of her hat.

"I don't get nervous . . . usually," Sarah says. But today, for reasons

she can't put her finger on, she feels a little edgy.

Naturally, Levi has picked up on this. He will be competing in some roping events, and perhaps to cover up his own nervousness, or perhaps because it is something brothers are supposed to do, he shares the story of one of Sarah's most spectacular barrel-racing disasters, which happened last year. "The horse turned real sharp and Sarah kept going forward."

Sarah laughs, remembering. "I just jumped off the horse."

"She looked so graceful," her step-grandmother adds. "Landed on her feet like she'd planned to get off her horse like that." Everybody laughs, which seems to keep nervousness at bay, at least for the moment.

The arena in Kalispell isn't full, but the crowd is enthusiastic. Sarah does well in barrel racing. Her horse hugs the barrels as she spins around them and streaks down the home stretch. She finishes in second place. In the breakaway calf-roping event, she and her horse shoot from the healer's box, rope loop circling, aimed for the little calf's neck. She lets go of the rope and misses the calf entirely, which puts her out of the competition.

Sarah is quietly disappointed with her performance, but there is not much time to linger over the triumphs or disappointments of today's

competition. The horses must be tended and loaded into the trailer. The drive home will take an hour or so. Chores will be waiting, and tomorrow Sarah will be back in school—not as a barrel racer, not as a calf roper, not as a rancher, but as an eighth-grader.

There is much to balance in Sarah's life—several communities in which to live. It's a little like having several full-time jobs. But Sarah seems to thrive on all of this, working each of her jobs with style.

As she spins around a barrel, Sarah's hair stays in place even though her hat flew off soon after the start.

A FAMILY THAT TAMES WINTER

Katy Whitlock, Wyoming

WINTER IN THE HIGH PLAINS of south-central Wyoming can be many things. It can bring surprises from the Wind River Range to the west, or it can come blasting down from the north. It can sneak in from the east or lumber up, heavy and wet, from the south.

It takes a family pulling together to make it through a Wyoming winter. And the Whitlock family is one that pulls together like a well-matched team of draft horses.

At the Whitlock ranch, tucked into the shallow Sweetwater River Valley halfway between Riverton and Rawlins, winter can be cows with frost-covered whiskers, thick as yarn, or wispy, sparkling snowflakes falling from a clear sky as the sun comes up. Winter is walking on snow with cornstarch squeaks and air so cold that the vapor from noses and mouths disappears before a breath can be completely exhaled.

For Katy Whitlock, winter is steam rising into the cold air from the warm water she uses to clean Clementine's teats in preparation for milking. Katy is gentle and calm, dipping the washcloth into the water and

Katy Whitlock's life is rich with family, animals, work, and fun.

wringing it out before wiping off the cow's bag (or udder) and wrapping the cloth around each teat, pulling downward. Clementine isn't always as relaxed and mellow as now. In fact, her hind feet are hobbled so she won't kick. "She knows when the water isn't warm enough," Katy says with a grin. She quickly coats the palm sides of her hands and fingers with sticky-smooth Corona salve, which makes it easier for her to slide her squeezing hands down each teat, and also prevents the teats from getting chapped.

Outside the milk shed, dawn has begun to stir, and fog in the river valley has frozen onto anything that doesn't move—clinging to willows, fences, trees, grass, and dozing animals. The result is hoarfrost that is thicker than the winter coats of horses and cattle. Also stirring are the barn cats, almost a dozen of them, who suddenly appear, loosely sur-rounding Katy and the milk cow, some crouched atop bales of hay and some perched on posts.

One cat, a smallish thirteen-year-old golden tiger, sits calm and col-lected under Clementine, behind the milk bucket. Her eyes shine. Her chin is raised, and her manners are as impeccable and dignified as the curve of her back. She is the oldest cat at the Whitlocks' ranch, the mother of most of the cats that have gathered, and a family favorite. As milk pings against the metal bottom of the milk bucket, this cat waits patiently for a squirt to come her way.

A cat waits patiently for a squirt or two of Clementine's warm milk.

She is not disappointed. After a half dozen squirts, the ping of milk against metal becomes the hiss of milk hitting milk, and Katy whispers, "Here you go," aiming the next stream at the cat.

The cat closes her eyes and opens her mouth, licking at the milk as fast as she can, but not fast enough. She starts gagging. Milk runs down her neck and chest. "She'll get cold," Katy says, squirting milk into an empty cat-food can that she has nudged from the straw with her foot. The cat comes over to the can and drinks while the other cats watch with hopeful intensity, both jealous and respectful.

Steam comes from each stream as it leaves the cow and gently rises from the foamy-headed milk. It doesn't take long for Katy to strip the last of the milk from Clementine. She uses the washcloth to wipe excess Corona salve from Clementine's teats and her own hands. She then hangs the bucket of milk on a high peg by the cow-shed door. Steam falls over the edge of the bucket, quickly disappearing. Katy grabs a pitchfork and tidies the shed, disposing of manure, before releasing Clementine's hobbles and directing the cow outside.

Katy walks to the house with the milk, passing her father, Bob, on his way to harness the workhorses. They smile at each other, Bob's smile shyly peeking out from under his thick, bushy mustache. Jack, the family's border collie, is dancing in front of Bob, eager to get on with the day's work.

Just inside the house, Katy walks through a cluster of younger siblings—her brother, Will, and two of her sisters, Shelly and Anna—who are pulling on their insulated jackets and work duds, including rubber boots and hats with furry earflaps. They are the family team designated to help their father feed cattle this morning. Before she can join them, Katy must strain the milk (almost two gallons) into jars that will sit in the refrigerator, letting the cream rise to the top for skimming off. After straining, the cheesecloth has no visible debris—bits of straw or hair or dirt—which is proof that Katy did a fine, clean job of milking.

WINTER

Soon Katy is back outside, over by the barn. Her father is finished hooking Squiggy and Laverne—large horses, Laverne being full-blooded Percheron and Squiggy being her son from a quarter horse—to the flatbed wagon, onto which the children have shoveled dried ears of corn for the cattle. Her father climbs aboard, joining Will, Shelly, and Anna. He takes the reins in his hands, and stands at the front of the wagon as he drives. Katy trots to the barbed-wire gate and drags it open for the wagon to pass through, then hooks it closed. Bob pulls the wagon to a stop as Katy climbs aboard to stand next to him.

Katy shows good form while opening a barbed-wire fence gate.

Away from the ranch buildings, the landscape opens up as if by magic. Naked red-tinted willow branches define the banks of the Sweetwater River, which loops westward. In this part of Wyoming, if you wait long enough to shovel snow, the wind will blow much of it away. The exposed tops of little hillocks look like waves riding a sea of white. Standing at the edge of this pasture, looking west, you can almost feel the gentle, rhythmic movements of the shallow ocean that once covered this vast plain.

To the north, up at the head of the bull pastures, are outcroppings made of brown-red rocks, each one looking like a huge loaf of bread. Many pioneers following the Oregon Trail came through a wide gap in these outcroppings more than a century ago. They would have recognized the leather creak of the Whitlocks' horse team and the wooden groans of the flatbed wagon.

Why, in this day of machines, does this ranching family use horses instead of trucks, tractors, or four-wheelers? Well, horses tend not to break down even if the "steering" sometimes has a mind of its own. And, sixty miles from a town, there are advantages to being self-sufficient, emancipated from the demands of oil and gas and mechanical breakdowns.

For Katy and her family, horses are a large part of what makes their way of life possible.

But watching Bob and the Whitlock children, one can sense deeper, more important reasons. There is a gentleness to the sounds and movements of the horses. Horses are part of the landscape—they could have been designed for it. Horses allow the Whitlocks to feel a deeper connection to this land that provides their livelihood.

Even more than all such highfalutin ruminating, the Whitlocks just plain love working with horses, dealing with the quirkiness of their personalities, trusting in their reliability.

The cold air makes the chains on the horse team ring as clearly as little silver bells as the wagon dips down the bank onto the river, across the snow-covered ice, and up the far bank. At this sound, the cattle in the pasture across the Sweetwater River begin to bawl in anticipation of food. But they will have to wait a few more minutes while Katy breaks ice at a watering hole in the river.

Katy hops down from the wagon and takes the ax from where it is stowed. As her father and siblings look on, she clomps down to the river, where an eye-shaped hole is sealed by a cornea of thin, glassy ice. One pop with the ax shatters this brittle seal, and in less than a blink, the shards disappear, carried under the six-inch-thick slab that covers the

Breaking ice in the river beats hauling water.

fast-flowing water. During the night, ice grew along the hole's rim, making it shrink with the cold. A few more whacks widen the hole to the permanent ring of dirt brought by the hooves of thirsty cattle. The grit of this dirt keeps animals and people from skidding into the gurgling water.

That chore done, Katy tromps back to the wagon, hands the ax to her father, and hops aboard. A flick of Bob's wrists telegraphs a signal through the reins to the alert horses. They break into a smart trot, Jack barking and prancing in front of them as if he were in charge, and begin to make a leisurely zigzag through the pasture while the kids kick and shove corn off the wagon bed. Some cattle stop and draw whole ears into their mouths with their sticky-looking, surprisingly nimble tongues. Others follow the wagon, bawling like calves after a mother. Soon the cows are spread throughout the pasture, heads bent toward corn that is scattered on the ground. The bawling stops. It is hard now to distinguish between the crunch of hooves on snow and the crunch of chewing.

Back across the river, near the barn, Bob brings the empty wagon to a stop next to a stack of hay bales. The kids hop up onto the hay and wrestle bales toward the wagon for the next phase of feeding. Bob guides the bales as they tumble down, arranging them on the wagon just so.

While the humans are loading hay, Jack makes himself "useful,"

playfully rearranging frozen cow chips and nosing one dropped ear of corn toward another one.

Bob is attentive as his kids struggle with the hay, but he doesn't interfere much, offering advice only when needed. "When they're little, it takes a lot more time to take the kids with you when you work. But it sure is worth it when they're older." He says this with pride as he watches them. His children are important to the running of the ranch, and this translates for each child into a sense of self-respect and satisfaction in a job well done.

As soon as the hay is loaded up, horses, wagon, and Whitlocks take off again for the far side of the river. As Bob cuts each bale's orange plastic twine, the kids shove flakes of hay overboard. Katy collects the twine, draping each length in the crook of her thumb. Her grandmother taught her how to hook baling twine into rugs that are perfect for wiping the mud from boots before coming inside.

By now the sun is strong enough to loosen the hoarfrost from whatever it clings to. Each time there is a puff of wind, the willows and the barbed wire look as if they were shedding clumps of hair. Cold as the air remains, wrestling with hay is hot work, and jackets are soon half unzipped.

Once the hay is unloaded, Bob drives the team back to the barn and

Katy heaves corn onto a flatbed wagon—the Whitlock family's version of physical education.

pulls up alongside a small hill of corn. The corn is good fodder for cows that will be calving in a month or so and, better yet, this year it wasn't any more expensive than hay. Of course, with last year's dry summer, hay was anything but cheap. Still, ranchers find good news in this business wherever possible.

As her father unhooks the harnessing and leads the horses away, Katy and her sisters grab scoop shovels and begin throwing corn onto the empty wagon. They are getting ready for tomorrow's cycle of feeding. Will, who will turn six in a couple of days, climbs the hill of corn and throws himself down it headfirst. "It's better than sledding. You don't get snow down your gloves," he says, climbing up for another slide.

Soon all the jackets are in a pile. Each shovelful of corn can weigh ten to fifteen pounds, and the flatbed is a little more than shoulder height. It's hot work.

"This is physical education class," Katy remarks with a grunt as she heaves corn into the wagon, pigtails flying. She's referring to the fact that she and her siblings are homeschooled, with their mother, Judy, serving as the teacher and principal rolled into one. Since they are an hour's drive from the nearest school, this makes sense to them. Judy and Bob believe the time that would be spent commuting is better used helping out on the ranch and doing schoolwork in the family's classroom—a separate room that is complete with desks in a row, chalkboard, textbooks, reference books, and an American flag.

How much corn goes onto the wagon? Katy thinks for a moment. "We shovel till it looks right," she says, with a look that is hard to read, both serious and joking.

Lunch is the biggest meal of the day. In the house now, work clothes shucked and hung in the mudroom, Katy, her sisters, and her brother walk into a kitchen that smells of bread baking. Whatever dough is left over becomes cinnamon raisin bread or other tasties.

Their mother has started making lunch. Katy prepares for making butter by pouring cream that has been skimmed from the milk into two large plastic jars. She then joins Shelly in peeling a couple dozen potatoes.

Katy's older sister, Becky, has been watching their youngest sister, Emily, who is two. Emily runs around and around the kitchen island counter where much of this is happening, underfoot and fussy because she's hungry. There are lots of hands to gently guide her from trouble. At the counter, sitting on aspen-wood stools, Anna and Will draw horses and brands. All the Whitlock children know the brands of surrounding ranches, and Will draws a series of them with obvious enthusiasm.

Three of the children have brands of their own, officially registered. Becky's is the F-Spear. Katy's is the Bar-7-Kay. Shelly's is called the Bog Knot because its ramp of connected C's looks like the lumps of bog soil that rise after freezing and thawing over and over in late winter and early spring. The other children will get their own brands as they get older.

The Whitlock family brands (left to right): F-Spear, Bar-7-Kay, Bog Knot, and Cross-Heart.

But the most important brand of all belongs to the family. Called the Cross-Heart, it is most appropriate for this tight-knit family whose hearts cross and recross as each day unfolds.

Every so often, as a break or between jobs, various family members wander over to the plastic jars of cream and give them a prolonged shaking. "It gets the nervousness out," Katy explains, shaking both at once. Before long a big lump of butter can be found in each jar, floating in buttermilk. Sometimes making butter takes less time, sometimes more. "If the kitchen is too cold, making butter takes forever . . . but it's better," Katy explains. "If the kitchen's too hot, butter doesn't form."

A few hard shakes later, Katy scrubs her hands carefully, hard enough so her skin blushes red. She takes the lump of butter from each jar and squeezes excess buttermilk from it. Next she rinses the butter in warm water (but not too warm), which gets rid of the rest of the

buttermilk. Switching to cold water, she lets the butter firm up. She adds salt to the butter (an amount that isn't measured, but that comes from experience) and kneads it in thoroughly. The butter is now ready to pack into an airtight container to chill and save. As for the buttermilk, it will be used to make pancakes for Sunday breakfast.

Lunch is ready, and the table is set for seven. Emily, in her high chair, makes eight. She may be only two, but already she is proving to be a no-nonsense eater, like her older brother and sisters and her parents— meat and potatoes, preferably.

One of the best cures for the winter doldrums is a taste or two of summer. Home-canned corn, home-canned beans, and homemade buffalo-berry jelly please the tongue and warm the tummy.

"In our garden we raise beans and corn and squash and zucchini and potatoes and root vegetables like carrots and beets," Katy says. "Because our growing season is so short we raise tomatoes and lettuce and such in our greenhouse." Indeed, their growing season is short. Katy's parents remember a year when it frosted on July 4 and again on July 13. Was one a late frost and the other an early frost? Who knows, but the odd freak frost in July can wreck a growing season and keep reminders of summer off the table in winter.

The boldest reminder of summer comes from the buffalo-berry

The Whitlocks always give thanks before meals—even little Emily.

jelly—like crab apple mixed with gooseberries, both tart and sweet, with a twist all its own—which tastes wonderful when spread with homemade butter on homemade bread fresh from the oven. Buffalo berries aren't easy to pick. "The bushes have thorns," says Katy. And you have to know

which buffalo-berry bush to pick from. "They're just like people. Some of them have sour berries and some have berries that are sweeter."

"The sour bushes are always sour, year in and year out," her father adds with a wry smile.

After lunch there is time for each member of the family to catch up with himself or herself. Katy retreats to her bedroom to finish sewing a birthday shirt for Will on her treadle sewing machine. "This is my cup of tea," she says, double-stitching a pocket that is likely to get a workout. "The electric sewing machines go so fast! And on these treadle machines, you can work your frustrations out." The rhythm of her speech echoes the rhythm of her pumping feet.

Other afternoons, she might hook rugs from baling twine, or work on her quilt, which she is filling with a batting made of cattail down she gathered in the fall. She might also tinker with the dollhouse that she has spent years building and furnishing—down to the place settings on the little tables. She smiles, fingering a railing that Emily has pulled loose and putting a doll back where it belongs. "It's a terrible thing when you know you're too old to play with dolls and you do anyway."

After an hour or so, the family gathers again for afternoon chores. Today the bulls need pellets. Katy, Will, and Anna volunteer. They put on their warm working clothes, catch and saddle their horses, and take off

Katy's bedroom is filled with things that she's made herself.

toward the stone outcroppings and the bull pasture. From the far end of the pasture, the bulls see them coming and gather around a horse trailer in which bags of pellets are stored. The bulls are remarkably gentle and calm as they stand, watching. Their wait is soon rewarded.

Jack, the family border collie, supervises as the Whitlock family gets ready to skate.

The sun is dropping as Katy, Will, and Anna finish unsaddling. The sky is turning the gray of frozen river ice, which is appropriate. The family grabs skates and heads for the river. Blown snow covers the spot they like to skate on, but the snow isn't very thick. Ripples in the ice,

hidden by the snow, make skating much more interesting. As Bob clears a section of ice with a shovel, the snow comes up in wind-packed chunks that are perfect for throwing. Will loses little time grabbing snow and heaving it at his sisters, who join in the fun. Bob finally gives up shoveling—thrown snow covers the ice faster than he can clear it. And then he joins the fracas, chuckling as he shows his kids a thing or two about dodging snowballs and good aim.

• • •

The next day, after morning chores and school, is an educational field trip for the whole family: a bull auction. Bob needs a couple more bulls for his herd, so they hook up the livestock trailer (just in case), pile into the double-cab truck, and head for the Riverton Livestock Auction Sale Barn.

The whole family inspects the bulls, which are in a maze of pens outside. Bob makes notes on the auction program about several possible purchases. Inside the arena, the family sits together and watches as the bulls are presented. Bob's notes remind him what he thinks potential purchases are worth, and he doesn't get caught up in the heady competition of bidding—he never bids a dollar more than what he plans to bid.

The kids take a deep interest in the bulls, especially those their

father bids on. They are learning, not by asking questions but by being alert and observant. They watch with an intensity other kids might show at a close basketball game. When the auction is over, their family owns two new bulls.

This purchase is important, and the entire family seems to relax now that it is done. If chosen well, these new bulls will improve the quality of the Whitlocks' herd. The children won't know how good their father's choices were until next winter, and then only by judging the quality of the new bulls' offspring.

Calving will begin this year in a little over a month, late February or early March. "I love calving," Katy says. Because she is an early-morning person (often doing schoolwork in the quiet of the house before breakfast), she usually gets the early shift—watching the cows in the calving pens to make sure they don't have problems giving birth, and also watching for predators who are attracted by the smell of blood and afterbirth (mainly coyotes, who whelp around calving time). For most cows, calving is done privately and without fanfare, usually when people are not about.

Tomorrow night the Whitlocks will be back at the Sale Barn, breathing in the smell of cow flops and urine. Instead of listening to the auctioneer and the bawling and snorting of bulls, they will be listening to a preacher who comes once a month for Saturday-evening cowboy church

services. Sunday-morning services would interfere with chores, which cannot be skipped, even for church.

The Whitlocks will sit together, sing together, and pray together in the arena with the same easy intensity they show while working together in the middle of a Wyoming winter.

Winter in Wyoming may be tough. But it is no match for the Whitlock family.

RANCH TIME IN THE SPRINGTIME

Leslie Barmann, New Mexico

I N THE KITCHEN, Leslie Barmann is yawning and looking for her boots. It's early according to her watch—at least an hour before sunrise—but she knows that watches don't tell ranch time. Unlike school, the day doesn't start at a certain hour. It starts when there's work to be done.

People time and ranch time. Two different ways to travel through a day and through a year, one of them pushing and prodding, the other leading on a generous rein.

Some people measure the seasons by flipping the pages of a calendar. Ranchers measure them by the look of their grasslands and cattle.

On a ranch, spring doesn't arrive until it announces itself.

"I know it's spring when the miller moths take over the house," says Leslie's mother, Kim, manager of the Clayton Place, which is part of her family's CS Ranch. Kim is frying up bacon and eggs and frowning at the moths batting against the reflection of kitchen light on the night-dark windows. It happens every year, usually in May but not always—a few weeks after the last freeze of the winter and a few weeks before the flies

Leslie loves being in the thick of branding action each spring.

get so bad they make the horses and cattle go a little crazy.

It's sure-enough spring now because, aside from the moths, there's a branding to get ready for. This morning, over three hundred calves will experience the noisy, smelly, confusing, sometimes bloody, sometimes painful, always terrifying things that calves have experienced for five generations of Leslie's family on this sprawling ranch outside Springer, New Mexico, a town named after her great-great-granduncle.

Kim slides the fried eggs onto plates, where they push up against strips of bacon. Leslie and her sister, Kelly, carry the plates into the dining room and slide into their chairs. Kim follows with a stack of toast. Smiles come easier as everyone eats. Conversation is punctuated by mouthfuls.

"Just take the plates to the sink, sweetie," Kim calls from the mud-room. But Leslie is ahead of her. She's already headed for the kitchen, plates stacked in her hands, silverware rattling on top.

Outside, a breeze rustles the shadowy leaves of giant cottonwoods that surround and shelter the ranch house. Nobody says anything—this is not a time for words, but a time for clearing the head of sleepy thoughts and thinking about the day.

Leslie walks past her father's truck—he'll head for work at the paving company he owns in an hour or so—to her mother's truck. Its cab

serves as a mobile ranch office, filled with coils of rope (known as hard twist) for roping, bottles of serum for inoculations, and various odds and ends of ranching equipment—there isn't much room inside for both girls. Walking around to the back of the truck, she and her sister sit on the lowered tailgate. Side by side, they swing their legs, kicking at the dust that rolls up from under the truck as their mother drives a mile or so to the branding pens.

The girls jump off the tailgate before the truck comes to a full stop. Several miller moths pop from the cab when Kim opens the door and hops out. She doesn't notice. The engine has stopped, but its rumble-purr is not replaced by quiet. The surrounding sounds are constant but calm—meadowlarks trilling, three corralled horses nickering nearby, and, to the west, a scattered herd of cows and calves that were branded last week calling to one another, sounding content. The still air is cool but not cold.

The top of the sun breaks through a low cloud as Kim, Leslie, and Kelly slip bridles onto their horses, which they trailered yesterday to one of the branding corrals and left overnight. Once they've saddled up and mounted, Kim and the girls head for pastures to the south and east.

The land feels vast and uncluttered. But if you look closely, you'll see faint seams that are made by fences. And wherever there are fences, there are gates.

"Gates are a pain," Leslie says. The ones in the corrals are cleverly designed to be opened and closed on horseback, but fence gates usually mean dismounting and remounting unless your horse is experienced and patient enough to help. Leslie stays on her horse—she's training him not to "booger" when she unhooks the barbed-wire gate. Her horse tries to back away at all the wrong times, skittish of the limp, floppy wire as she drags the gate open.

Kim and Kelly ride through. "Attagirl," Kim says encouragingly, as Leslie calmly and firmly pulls her horse's head in the right direction and gives him a tap-kick so that he moves backward and forward when she needs him to.

After Leslie rehooks the gate behind her, she and her mother and sister break into an easy trot. Three abreast, they drop into a draw, climb up the other side, and disappear over the rise beyond.

The sun gathers itself into a ball as it rises above the low cloud. A breeze kicks up, bringing with it warmer air. The day is going to be hot. With any luck, the branding will be done before the heat gets uncomfortable.

Several more trucks with trailers drive up to the corrals and holding pens. The hired hands and an assortment of Leslie's relatives have

Leslie checks her sister Kelly's saddle.

come with their horses to help bring in the cattle and to brand. There are no words spoken—it's just too early. The only sounds are the clanging of trailer gates opening and the pounding of hooves on wooden trailer floors as the saddled horses back out. Soon these horses and riders are headed over the same rise Leslie went over.

This next leisurely stretch of ranch time will contain the last tranquility of the morning. For anyone waiting behind, sitting on a corral fence and wearing a cowboy hat, the sun rises enough to disappear over its brim. The breeze kicks a little harder. And then a thin mist lifts above the rise.

At first it looks like steam being drawn from the earth by the sun. The faint sound of bawling fills the air. Rising from the earth is a fine dust, kicked up by a herd of cattle on the move.

The bawling grows more intense. Suddenly cows and calves spill over the rise. Gamboling calves dart in and out of the ragged phalanx of advancing cows. Some of the cows stumble slightly as they crane their necks backward to call for lagging calves. The dust is carried on the breeze, seasoned now by the nervous smell of cow flops. One calf was standing at the wrong end of a cow at the wrong time, and it shakes its head as it skips along, trying to get rid of the slippery green-brown stuff that drips down its face.

Like mother, like daughters: Kim, Kelly, and Leslie ride tall in the saddle, holding their reins with confidence.

First Leslie, and then Kim and Kelly, appear over the rise. Leslie is waving a hand, controlling the left flank of the herd, going back and forth behind them at an easy lope. Kim and Kelly are joined by three other riders, who are helping sweep up loose cattle that bolted from the herd, darting between horses.

The bawling has grown frantic by now. With bulging eyes that show white, calves tip their snouts up and bleat for their mothers. Mothers arch their necks toward the sky and bugle for their babies.

The sound of a frightened cow gives the impression that its head must be hollow. Cows may not have much in the way of brains, but put all the little brains in a herd together and they can cause wrecks—horses colliding with horses, cattle with cattle, or horses with cattle. When that happens animals and riders can be hurt, maybe even trampled. Horses and riders must be alert to the unpredictable movements of cattle and react calmly and with authority before the cows and calves get out of hand. More than one branding has been delayed an hour or two because the herd splintered and stampeded in several directions.

There aren't any wrecks today. In fact, some of the cattle are so calm that their calves walk along nosing stalks of grass, tongues darting out to twiddle with them, but not eating. These calves are still nursing—they won't eat grass for several months—and some of them are even wobbly-legged from being herded, having been born less than a week ago.

With a large holding pen full and one hired hand headed back out to search for any stragglers, the branding is ready to begin. Friends and neighbors are arriving, their pickups parked in a cluster with noses stuck into the shade of nearby elm trees. Brandings are community affairs, a chance to help neighbors who have helped you at one time or another.

For those whose most intimate encounter with cattle lies flattened

between hamburger buns, what exactly is a branding? Leslie thinks for a moment before answering. She's been around brandings all her life, and it's hard to explain something so obvious. "Well, it's where you take the calves and you just rope them and flank them and mark them and inoculate them and, if it's a male, you cut them." She smiles, as if to say, "It's that simple."

It may seem simple to her, but to someone watching for the first time, a branding can seem too chaotic to make sense. By marking the calves, Leslie not only means branding them with a hot iron, but cutting distinctive notches in both ears to claim them for her family's CS Ranch. The calves should already have bright plastic tags with numbers fastened to their ears. These are not a rancher's idea of the latest in bovine jewelry, but are used to record the age of each calf and its mother. If a calf doesn't have an ear tag, it will get one while being branded.

By cutting the males, she means castrating them. With a very sharp pocketknife, each bull calf's scrotum is cut open, and the two testicles are popped out and severed with the blade. Surprisingly, this causes very little bleeding.

In less than thirty seconds, a bull calf becomes a steer. Each about the size of a thumb, the testicles are not fully formed. In most cases, they are still tucked away inside the calf's body cavity and must be popped out

with fingers pressing on either side of the scrotum, which itself is nothing more than puckery skin and not yet stretched out like the sac of a bull. Because of this, if done swiftly and cleanly, castration isn't as painful as it looks.

Castration is done for good reason—without testicles the calf's meat won't grow tough from the male hormone testosterone, which is produced in the testicles.

Marking and cutting are not yet jobs for Leslie and Kelly. From the very first calf to the last, they will be in charge of inoculations. But before Leslie and Kelly can do their jobs, each calf must be caught.

It would be difficult to say which of their older relatives are most masterful at roping. They've been at it a long time. Each one of them has a distinct style, and each is accurate, usually slipping the rope's loop around the hind legs of a calf on the first throw.

Roping a calf takes concentration and finesse, and both the horse and rider must be alert. The horse must be aware of all the cattle milling around its legs and must also focus on whatever commands come from its rider's legs and hands. The rider must "read" the horse, and also concentrate on moving into a position behind a particular calf that will

Leslie helps control a feisty calf.

increase the odds of a successful throw to its hind legs, which must both be off the ground. The work of a well-trained horse and experienced rider is a pleasure to watch: a couple of smart sidesteps, several swings of the rope's loop, a toss, the swirl of flying rope, a jerk, and—bingo!—the calf's hind legs are neatly bound. Almost immediately, the horse pulls back to take in the rope's slack. The calf falls forward as the hind legs are lifted in the air. Sometimes the calf paws the ground, frantic to get away, too startled to cry out as it's dragged a few feet toward one of the two branding stations.

The first two people to greet each calf are the flankers. The rear flanker drops the calf onto its left side and then loosens and removes the rope. Almost simultaneously, this flanker sits right behind it facing forward, his feet pushing the calf's bottom rear leg, leaning back while gripping and pulling the top leg like an oar of a rowboat. By doing this, the rear flanker exposes the belly of the calf, making it easy to determine its sex and, if it is male, to make the work of the castrater convenient and quick.

The front flanker faces the rear flanker and works at the calf's shoulders, leaning into the neck, controlling the head, and keeping the calf from scrambling onto its front legs.

Even before the calf is on the ground and stretched out, yet another person has grabbed a red-hot CS branding iron from the flame of one of two propane torches. If the calf is male, Leslie's uncle Randy is kneeling, stretching the skin of the scrotum, preparing to cut. Some calves continue struggling after they hit the ground, but others give up, panting, tongues lolling, eyes rolled back, trying to glimpse the monsters surrounding them.

While this is happening, Leslie and Kelly are standing behind their respective calves at their separate stations, yellow inoculation guns at the ready. In inoculating, as in most ranching jobs, timing is everything. The branding iron hits the calf's ribs, followed by an explosion of smoke from burning hair and a sudden bellow of surprise from the calf. Sometimes the hair around the iron catches fire, but the fire goes out as fast as it flares. Even before the smoke clears, Leslie and Kelly crouch by their respective calves' shoulders, place the inoculation guns at just the right angle against the nape of the neck, punch the needles through hide (but not muscle), squeeze the triggers to release the right amount of serum, and pull the needles out.

Both Leslie and Kelly are the perfect size to slip in and do their job without interfering with flankers, castraters (who also notch the ears), or branders. If they are fast enough, they are standing once more behind the calf they've just inoculated as a single-number branding iron

(corresponding to the last number in the year) has finished marking a female (but not male) calf on its hip.

"Inoculating is a lot of fun." Leslie grins. "The trick is trying not to stick the flankers." Of course she's joking, but inoculating is not without its dangers. A writhing calf can sometimes slip out from under the front flanker, which puts the rear flanker and the inoculator in danger of getting stuck or kicked. It has happened to Leslie: the needle of her inoculation gun narrowly missed a flanker, piercing his denim jeans before piercing the calf's hide.

After inoculation, the branding team releases each calf, which scrambles to its feet and wobbles to the far side of the branding corral.

For five straight hours, Leslie and Kelly will do their jobs, jumping in at precisely the right time and then jumping out, taking a break only to practice flanking with smaller calves.

"Boys sometimes think they can do the tougher jobs and that I can't. But I can flank," Leslie says. "And I'm tough." She rubs her left shoulder where a calf's hind foot slammed against her when the front flanker, a boy cousin, lost control. "I have a bruise to prove it."

Toward the end of the morning, when everybody is moving more slowly, the girls can talk and joke around with their cousins, who wait for their turns to practice flanking. The sound of crying cattle is just as loud

Leslie jumps in at just the right time to inoculate a calf.

as before, as is the hiss of the propane torches' flames, but now they are able to tune out the sounds. It's the smells that are impossible to tune out. "The smell of burning skin and hair is hideous," Leslie says, wrinkling her nose.

Finally the last calf is branded. The propane torches are turned off, and the cattle are turned out to pasture. Almost immediately, the intensity of

the bawling begins to die down as cows find their calves. Within an hour each calf will be reunited with its mother. Right away it will start to nurse, and peacefulness will return to the ranch.

Everybody who helped at the branding—aunts, uncles, cousins, hired hands, neighbors, friends—gathers at an old Santa Fe Railroad caboose that sits under a nearby grove of Chinese elms. The caboose is miles from the closest railroad tracks but only a stone's throw from the actual (but faint) wagon-wheel ruts of the famous Santa Fe Trail, first linking Independence, Missouri, to Santa Fe, New Mexico, in the nineteenth century. Leslie's grandmother has prepared lunch for everyone. Among other things, she's serving meatloaf because one old hand refuses to wear his false teeth, claiming they feel as comfortable as a bear trap in his mouth.

Brandings are hard work, but after the work is done there is time for visiting and kidding around. It's already been a long day for Leslie. It's tempting to linger in the shade, have another cup of iced tea, kick back, visit, and declare the day's work done.

But the needs of a ranch aren't organized around the whims of ranchers. Ranchers organize their lives around the needs of the ranch. There are 4-H lambs that need feeding and attention, a dehydrated calf in the barn, and a week-old foal that needs an injection of antibodies. On

Lunch after a branding is one part food, two parts conversation.

top of that, somebody driving to the branding that morning spotted a wobbly calf in a far pasture. It might be sick or abandoned by a confused first-time mother.

So in a practical sense, the branding notwithstanding, the day is

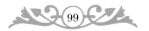

only beginning. After lunch, Leslie helps her mother and sister load their horses into the trailer and head for home.

● ● ●

"This one's a bruiser," Leslie says, kneeling beside her male lamb, holding his neck in the crook of her arm. As she slips a halter on him, he jerks his head, trying his best to flip it off. "But he's fun to mess around with." When the lamb kicks out with his sharp front feet, it becomes clear that lambs may be as soft and cute as plush toys, but you wouldn't want to sleep with one on your bed.

It's more fun than work to prepare lambs for showing at the county fair. Lambs are playful and energetic and bursting with personality. To prepare them for show, Leslie holds them, gets them used to a halter, and trains them to lead. She plays with them to make them feel comfortable with people, feeding them pellets and then cleaning up the rounder, darker pellets that come out the other end.

"We have to start jumping them soon," Leslie explains. "That's so they'll build up the muscles in their hindquarters."

By building up those muscles, Leslie means developing more meat for what butchers call "leg of lamb."

Leslie enjoys messing around with her 4-H lambs, training them to lead.

Is it hard to think of her lamb as mutton? Leslie's lamb has dropped onto its front knees and is nibbling selected greens from a patch of grass. Leslie nods. "It's hard to let the lambs go off to slaughter." She shrugs, as if to say, "But that's ranch life."

Even though the lambs are less than three months old, they will be headed for sale and slaughter in another three or four months. On a ranch there is always the danger of becoming too fond of an animal that may someday appear as food on your table. But it's hard not to grow fond of animals that are as cute and mischievous as lambs.

Leslie sees her mother headed from the house to the barn. She's carrying a plastic bladder of a rehydrating electrolyte solution she's just made in the kitchen, and a feeding tube. Kelly and Leslie try to hurry their lambs back into the barn, which makes the lambs fight their halters all the more.

"She looks a little better," Kim calls from the next stall, as Leslie and Kelly drag their lambs into the barn. The calf has had diarrhea for several days and hasn't been able to nurse enough to replenish its lost fluids. It missed out on the branding, and the stall smells rank where the calf has been lying, fouling the straw. "Could you hold her while I work this in? Watch out for the momma," Kim adds.

The mother cow is naturally protective and isn't happy to have

people around her calf, especially because the calf is too weak to stand. Kelly keeps an eye on her, but the cow stays off to the side while Leslie holds the calf around the neck and Kim slips a couple feet of plastic tubing down the calf's throat, all the way to its stomach. The calf is too weak to struggle.

Leslie and Kelly watch intently, learning, as Kim gently squeezes the electrolyte solution into the calf's stomach and pulls the tube out. "That'll do it," she says, as if her confidence will help the calf get better. If it doesn't, the calf will be hauled, like all dead animals on the ranch, to a pit down by the Cimarron River.

That done, Kim turns to Leslie and Kelly. "Let's go check out that wobbly calf." The three of them head for Kim's truck. Both Leslie and Kelly know which calf their mother is talking about.

Sitting on the tailgate, Leslie and Kelly are bounced by an unexpected bump. They giggle and hold on tighter. That's ranch life for you, which is never boring—even without television. The ranch is too remote to get reception without a satellite dish, which the family doesn't have. "You're always doing something," Leslie says, "in the house, or out of the house."

The truck goes over a cattle guard. Does she ever feel deprived, living on a ranch thirty miles from school and the town of Cimarron, where most of her friends live?

There are always calves to bring back to the herd.

Leslie shrugs. "It's sometimes hard, not seeing my friends enough. But I feel pretty lucky. I love the animals, being with my family, spending time with Mom . . ."

The sun seems to be picking up speed as it dips toward the western mountains. Shadows are longer. The heat of the day has lost its edge.

"Hey, Mom," Leslie calls, pointing toward a group of cattle. "That it?"

"I think so," her mother calls in answer.

SPRING

The truck turns off the dirt road and bucks once before settling down.

Is another spring day on the CS Ranch winding down? Perhaps. But only when it's good and ready. After all, around here it's ranch time that rules.